VIKINGS IN 30 SECONDS

First published in the UK in 2017 by Ivy Kids.
This edition published in the US in 2017 by

Ivy Kids

An imprint of The Quarto Group
The Old Brewery
6 Blundell Street
London N7 9BH
United Kingdom
www.QuartoKnows.com

ISBN: 978-1-78240-531-3

This book was conceived, designed & produced by

Ivy Kids

58 West Street, Brighton BN1 2RA, United Kingdom

PUBLISHER	Susan Kelly
CREATIVE DIRECTOR	Michael Whitehead
COMMISSIONING EDITOR	Hazel Songhurst
MANAGING EDITOR	Susie Behar
PROJECT EDITOR	Judith Chamberlain-Webber
ART DIRECTOR	Hanri van Wyk
DESIGNER	Suzie Harrison
EDITORIAL ASSISTANT	Lucy Menzies

Printed in China

10 9 8 7 6 5 4 3 2 1

VIKINGS
IN 30 SECONDS

PHILIP STEELE

ILLUSTRATED BY STEF MURPHY
CONSULTANT: DR. RAGNHILD LJOSLAND

IVY KIDS

Contents

About this book
... in 60 seconds

Around 1,200 years ago, many families along the coasts of northern Europe lived in fear. They stared out to the horizon, looking for the sails of unknown ships. Rumors spread like wildfire. People said that these ships carried armed raiders who attacked towns and villages and burned down churches. They were stealing treasure and murdering people or carrying them off to become slaves.

The raiders came from Scandinavia, the region of northern Europe now made up of Denmark, Sweden, and Norway. People called them Northmen and many other names. Today we generally call them Vikings. Soon these Vikings were attacking many other European countries.

The Vikings are often remembered as fierce warriors, with scary names like Eirik Bloodaxe, Thorfinn Skullsplitter or Ragnar Hairy Breeches. But, they should also be remembered because they were great traders, seafarers, and explorers. They were farmers, blacksmiths, jewelers, and skilled carvers of wood, stone and walrus tusk. They were poets, storytellers, and lawmakers.

Archeologists have discovered hoards of Viking treasure. They have excavated a magnificent ship that was used as the tomb of a noblewoman, who was wearing a fine red dress. They have uncovered entire towns, farm buildings, forts, and ports. Even garbage dumps and toilets can tell us a lot about how people used to live in the Viking age.

It's time to meet the Vikings. Every topic in this book has a page to read as fast or as slow as you like. If you are in a real hurry, you can read the 3-second sum-up instead. Each full-page illustration supplies a colorful, at-a-glance guide, too. Then, if you have a spare few minutes, there are extra facts to discover and exciting hands-on activities to try.

Lands and peoples

The Vikings lived in northern Europe during the Middle Ages from around 790 to 1050 CE. The Vikings developed from bands of raiders to become a powerful force in Europe. They were also great explorers, always looking to find new places to live. In about 800 CE, when their sea raids were beginning to spread fear, the map of Europe looked very different from today. Much of France, Germany, and Italy was ruled by an emperor called Charlemagne, who belonged to the Frankish people. Greece and areas of southeastern Europe were part of the Byzantine Empire. Britain and Ireland were made up of small kingdoms ruled by the Welsh, Scots, Picts, Anglo-Saxons, and Irish.

Lands and peoples
Glossary

amber A brown, yellow, or orange fossil, that is used in making jewelry.

Arctic Circle The ocean and lands that surround the North Pole and where there is midnight sun at midsummer.

assembly A public meeting or gathering.

bog iron An impure form of the iron that occurs naturally in the water of some marshes and swamps.

Byzantine Empire Lands ruled from the ancient city of Byzantium, which became Constantinople (and is now called Istanbul). It was originally the eastern part of the Roman Empire.

feud A long-lasting quarrel between two people or two families.

fjord (say "fiord") A deep-sea inlet in the coast, long and narrow with steep sides.

Frankish Of the Franks, a people living in France during the early Middle Ages. They gave their name to the country.

glacier A river of thick, very slow-moving ice.

jarl A rich and powerful nobleman, who was a member of the top class in Viking society.

karl A free male citizen in Viking society, able to own property and trade.

Middle Ages/medieval The period of European history that separates the time of ancient Rome from the modern world of discovery and science. Some historians date it from 476 CE to 1453.

Old Norse The language spoken by the Vikings.

ore Rock containing useful minerals, such as iron or gold.

outlaw Someone condemned at a trial to be cast out from society and refused the protection of the law.

pagan Someone who follows a pre-Christian or non-Christian faith.

rune One of the sticklike letters used in Viking alphabets.

Sami A people also known as Lapps. They live in the north of Norway, Sweden, Finland, and Russia.

thrall A Viking slave.

Homeland

... in 30 seconds

The Vikings originally came from Scandinavia—a region of mountains, forests, lakes, and bogs in northern Europe. Its long coastline is broken up by deep inlets, headlands, and islands. Some Vikings lived near the coasts, where there were harbors for ships and plentiful fish. Others lived in the flatlands of the south where crops could be grown.

The Vikings made their homes in scattered settlements and villages. Later, they built towns and forts. They mostly lived by farming and trading. Scandinavia could offer plenty of timber, furs, and minerals such as bog iron, a useful metal ore that could easily be collected from wetlands. Amber, a yellow or brown fossil resin, was valued for making jewelry.

Although Scandinavia was a good place to live, the Vikings wanted more land. Many wanted to get rich, by trading overseas or by attacking and looting distant lands. Some wanted to find better farmland where they could build new homes, or win power and fame. Above all, Vikings were adventurers. They loved sailing off to explore and settle new lands such as Iceland and Greenland.

3-second sum-up

The Vikings came from Scandinavia, where they lived by fishing, farming, and trading.

Timeline

Vendel Period (about 550–790s CE): This is the time before the Viking age, and all Viking customs and trading have their roots in this period. It takes its name from a place in Sweden.

Viking Age (790s–960 CE): These years mark the high point of the Viking way of life. It was a time of overseas raiding and settlement, long-distance exploration and trade.

Christian nations (about 960–1100 CE): During this time, Christianity gradually spreads through the Viking lands and larger, more powerful kingdoms grow up.

The Vikings lived in Scandinavia, which is a partly mountainous region of northern Europe.

Winters in the north were dark and bitterly cold and people needed wood for fires to keep warm.

Lakes and forests provided fish and timber.

Most of the Viking population lived in the southern regions of Scandinavia, where it was warmer, and along the coasts where they could easily sail.

Southern farmland had warm summers but snowy winters.

N
W
S

Who were the Vikings?

... in 30 seconds

"Vikings" is the name we give to people living in Scandinavia between about 1,200 and 900 years ago. They were the ancestors of today's Danes, Swedes, Norwegians, and Icelanders. The Vikings were related to other peoples living to the south, in Germany, and to those Anglo-Saxons who had settled in England. Some non-Viking peoples—ancestors of today's Sami—lived in Scandinavia, too.

During this time, the Vikings were known as "Northmen" or "Danes," or sometimes these raiders from afar were called pirates, pagans (non-Christians) or foreigners. All Vikings shared a similar background and way of life, but there were probably local differences in their customs or what they wore.

Despite speaking differently in different parts, they all used the same language called Old Norse. Over the centuries, as Vikings invaded and settled in other parts of Europe, Old Norse developed into some of the languages spoken in northern Europe today.

The Vikings wrote words down using letters called runes. However, at the end of the Viking Age, Norse began to be written in the Roman alphabet used in other parts of western Europe.

3-second sum-up

The Vikings spoke a language called Old Norse and wrote with letters called runes.

3-minute mission Crack the code!

The Viking alphabet is called the "futhark," which is the sound of its first six runes. Only 16 runes were used during Viking times.

ᚠᚢᚦᛆᚱᚴ ᚼᚾᛁᛆᛋ ᛏᛒᛘᛚᛌ

f u t h a r k   h n i a s   t b m l R

Can you translate these runes into modern English?

ᚦᛁᛋ ᚠᛁᛋᚴ ᛁᛋ ᛆ ᛋᚴᛆᚱᚠ
ᚦᛆᛏ ᛁᛋ ᛁᛏᛋ ᚠᛁᛆ

14

See page 96 for answers.

The name "Viking" may once have been linked to a part of the Norwegian coast known as Viken, but it soon became used to describe a pirate way of life.

Vikings often attacked other people to get more land or steal possessions. The word "Vikingr" meant going off on a voyage or raid. "Vikingar" (Vikings) could refer to those people taking part in a raid.

Vikings carved letters called runes to tell people important messages.

All Vikings shared a similar way of life and were great craftsmen and warriors.

Society

... in 30 seconds

Viking society was divided up into different groups or classes. At the top was the king. The first Viking kings were not grand rulers living in palaces. They often controlled quite small regions. Their power depended on wealth, success in war and keeping order, and support from their followers. Toward the end of the Viking Age, kings became more powerful and ruled over whole countries.

Viking noblemen came next and were called jarls (earls). They were rich and powerful owners of large areas of land, horses, and ships. They were expected to send warriors to support their king in battle.

Most Vikings were called karls, meaning freemen. Some were wealthy and owned land and houses, while others were poor. Karls might work as farmers, skilled craftsmen, blacksmiths, shipbuilders, or merchants. Most of the warriors, seafarers, and settlers were karls.

At the bottom were thralls (slaves), who were forced to work very hard as laborers or servants. They had few rights. Many slaves were captured during sea raids. Only a few were lucky enough to win or buy their freedom.

3-second sum-up

Viking kingdoms were divided into three main classes—nobles (jarls), freemen (karls), and slaves (thralls).

Women's world

Men ruled, but women were respected and had some rights. They needed to be tough and practical. It was the women who ran farms and homes while the men were away fighting. Women controlled the household budget and carried the keys to buildings and stores. Women were skilled spinners and weavers. They played an important part as pioneers settling new lands.

There was a strict order of society (hierarchy), with the king at the top and slaves at the bottom.

The king was expected to be brave. He was also expected to be generous to his followers in return for their loyalty.

Jarls were powerful chieftains who might organize raids or trading expeditions and command many warriors.

Karls were free citizens, with the right to own land and trade. Most karls were farmers.

Thralls were slaves who had to work very hard for their masters.

Law and order

... in 30 seconds

The Vikings had a strong sense of honor and they could be easily offended. Insults or crimes often ended in revenge and fighting, or in quarrels between families or individuals. These feuds could go on for many years.

Such problems might need to be sorted out at a public assembly, known as the Thing. Assemblies could settle arguments about property, marriage, and divorce. They could question witnesses about cases of murder, injury, or robbery. They could pass sentences, make new laws, or even proclaim someone king.

Each assembly covered a district or a region and was held at a particular time of the year. Assemblies were gatherings of free men only. Women and slaves could not take part in the assembly, but the interests of some women could be represented. The arrangements varied from one Viking land to another. In Iceland, people met at a place called the Assembly Plain, and gathered by the Law Rock. There, a council of chieftains was held to appoint a legal expert or "lawspeaker."

Assemblies could not carry out the sentences they passed, as there was nothing like a police force. It was up to the victims of the crime and the public to make sure that the law was enforced.

3-second sum-up

Public assemblies were held to pass laws and judge crimes.

Ancient parliaments

Viking assemblies were an early form of a parliament. Some of them still exist today. The Tynwald is a parliament on the Isle of Man, one of the British Isles that was settled by the Vikings. It has been meeting for over a thousand years. The Althing is the parliament of Iceland and has been passing laws since it was founded in 930 CE, aside from a gap in the 1800s when it was abolished, then reinstated.

Arguments and problems were figured out at a public assembly known as the Thing.

Men would gather from all over the region.

A thief might have to pay money back to his victim, as compensation.

The lawspeaker proclaimed the Viking law before the assembly.

A criminal could be exiled to a foreign land, or be declared an outlaw from society, with no rights.

Some disputes were settled by a "holmgang," which was armed combat between two people.

Seafarers

Many Vikings lived on coasts and islands, or beside rivers. Ships were often the quickest way to travel. People in Scandinavia had been building boats for a thousand years or more, and the Vikings were the best seafarers in Europe. The sea was their route to fame and fortune, and enabled them to raid and settle in unknown lands. Viking poets loved to write about the ocean. They thought up all sorts of clever names for it—such as the "whale-house," the "smooth path of ships," and the "slopes of the sea-king."

Seafarers
Glossary

awning A wide length of cloth used for shade or shelter.

barter To trade without money, by exchanging goods or services.

bazaar A busy market, generally under a roof, in the cities of western or southern Asia.

cargo Goods being carried by a ship.

clinker-built Having a hull made of overlapping planks.

crossbeam A ship's timber that joins and strengthens the two sides of the hull.

faering A small boat used for fishing or ferrying.

haggle To bargain over a trade deal.

helmsman The sailor who steers a ship.

hull The main body of a ship, its bottom and sides.

jetty A pier or quay where boats can be tied up.

karl A free male citizen in Viking society, able to own property and trade.

keel A wooden beam running along a ship's bottom and supporting the hull.

knarr A broad Viking ship designed to carry a lot of cargo.

longphort A Viking camp or base in Ireland.

longship A long and narrow Viking ship, used in raiding and exploration.

mint To make new coins, or the place where the coins are made.

monastery The buildings of a religious community, where monks live and worship.

navigate To plan a journey, following a course.

pagan Someone who follows a pre-Christian or non-Christian faith.

plunder To loot or steal goods using force; also the term for the goods obtained by looting and violence.

prow The projecting front part of a ship.

rib A strip of wood designed to strengthen the hull of a boat.

rivet A metal fastener or bolt, which holds together two wooden timbers or metal sections.

seafarer Someone who often travels by sea, such as a sailor.

starboard As you face forward, the right-hand side of a ship. (The left-hand side is known as the port side.)

stem The curved timber at the front of a ship that brings together the two sides of the hull.

stern The back end of a ship or boat.

strakes The planks of a ship's hull.

wind vane A flat piece of metal that moves to show the direction of the wind.

Making boats

... in 30 seconds

Building a Viking ship was very hard work. First, woodcutters chopped down trees in the forest. They stripped the trunks of their branches and then hauled them to a riverbank or shoreline. The best wood of all was oak, but ash, beech, or pine were useful, too.

Skilled carpenters cut and shaped the timbers with axes and scrapers. Some built the hull, using iron nails and rivets. Wool or animal hair soaked in tar was stuffed between the ship's planks, known as strakes, to keep them watertight.

Viking ships were powered by oars and sails. The rowers sat on wooden chests or on benches. The biggest ships had very long oars, and a broad steering oar or rudder lashed to the starboard side, toward the stern.

Large rectangular sails were generally made of woolen cloth. This was soaked in animal grease and possibly crisscrossed with strips of leather so that it could stand up to wind, rain, or spray from the sea. Sails could be colored or striped. Ropes made from twisted sealskin, horsehair, or plant fibers supported the mast and sails.

3-second sum-up

The Vikings built first-rate rowing boats and sailing ships.

Ship shapes

Small rowing boats called faerings might be used for a day's fishing. The knarr was a big ship, with some decking ore (front) and aft (back). It was broad and deep enough to hold cargo, horses, or cattle. It could be used for trading or settlement of new lands. The finest ship of all was the langskip or longship. It was slim and streamlined, ideal for long-distance raiding.

Axes are used to make wedge-shaped cuts in tree trunks.

These wedges will become the ship's strakes (planks).

The backbone of the ship is a long timber beam called the keel. It supports the hull.

The inside of the hull is strengthened with ribs and crossbeams.

The curved stem is at the front of the keel. It connects the two sides of the hull.

Viking ships were made very skillfully. They were clinker-built, which means that the planks of the hull overlapped each other.

The prow is tall and curved. Sometimes the wood is decorated with carvings.

The longship

... in 30 seconds

Just how long was a Viking longship? A typical vessel measured about 56 ft and had 16 or 18 oars on either side, with one man to each oar. Some of the later warships were much bigger, needing a crew of about 80 men. The keel of a warship found at Roskilde, in Denmark, was 105 ft. It dated from about 1025 CE.

The longship was designed for the open ocean. Its timbers were strong, but they could bend slightly with the motion of the waves. The hull was narrow and streamlined. Typical speeds ranged from about 5 to 10 knots (5.5—11.5 mph). The top speed would have been over 15 knots (17 mph).

Longships were light and were also designed for use in shallow water and rivers. This made it easy for raiders to jump ashore or haul the ship onto a beach.

These ships were also perfect for raiding, but did not have enough space to carry much extra cargo. They were not heavy enough to ram other ships, either. For an ocean battle, several ships had to be lashed together to provide a fighting platform. Shields were sometimes slotted along the side of the ship for display or protection.

3-second sum-up

Longships were long, narrow, and light. They were good in shallow waters as well as on the ocean.

3-minute mission Design a longship prow

The Vikings were great woodcarvers, and they liked to decorate their best ships. Sometimes the prow of a longship was carved in the shape of a beast, a snake, or a dragon. Its snarling jaws may have been intended to terrify the enemy or drive away evil spirits, or just impress other Vikings! You can design your own scary beast for a prow. Draw an outline on craft paper and cut it out. Draw in the detail.

A longship can be powered by sail or oars. The crew must be ready for storms, rough seas, or enemy attacks.

The mast could be unstepped (taken down) if necessary.

The helmsman steered the ship using his broad steering oar as a kind of rudder.

The carved dragon prow was designed to scare the enemy or evil spirits.

Oars might be 16–26 ft long.

Decking was loose. It could be easily raised if the ship took on water and needed bailing out.

On a voyage

... in 30 seconds

Longships were open boats, with no cabins. This meant that on a voyage the crew had to put up with salty ocean spray, icy winds, or burning hot sun, during hour after hour of hard rowing. A large cloth or awning could be put up to shelter the rowers. This could be taken ashore, along with tents, to set up a camp.

Personal weapons, cloaks, and food could be kept dry in the crew's sea chests. Dried or salted meat and fish, apples, nuts, and cheese were all easily stored foods that could last through a voyage. Fresh fish could be caught on the way, and shore visits could be used for hunting or taking on freshwater.

Viking crews didn't have good maps. They often followed coastlines, looking out for familiar features such as capes. At sea, they could check currents or movements of birds. They also looked at the positions of the Sun and stars. Raiding in summer months avoided darkness and winter storms.

Although longships were well built, they could still get caught by gales and giant waves, so shipwrecks were common.

3-second sum-up

Longships were open to the weather and the rowing was hard. The Vikings navigated by the Sun and stars.

3-minute mission Make a wind vane

You need: • Stiff cardboard • Scissors • Gold acrylic paint • Paintbrush • Black marker • A wooden stick • Tape
1. Draw a right angle on the cardboard, with the horizontal line measuring 4 in and the vertical one 2.5 in.
2. Draw a curved shape from one line end to the other (see drawing above). Cut out the curved shape and paint it gold.
3. When it's dry, use a marker to draw on snakes, lions, dragons, or birds. Then you can tape the short side to a stick and push it loosely into the ground. Watch the wind blow it around!

Voyages could take a week or two, so the crew needed supplies of food and freshwater.

Watching birds could help Vikings locate land, currents, and fishing grounds.

Wind vanes were put at the top of the mast to show which way the wind was blowing. They may also have served as emblems, to show which ship was leading the fleet.

Crews looked out for landmarks and the position of the Sun.

Vikings had to survive on dried or salted food, or fresh fish if they could catch them.

Ports and traders

... in 30 seconds

Viking merchants sailed around northern coasts, selling and buying goods, in knarrs, which were wide, deep ships with room for cargo. Viking ports such as Hedeby, in what is now Germany, had jetties where merchant ships could tie up. Viking traders sailed or rowed up rivers, too. If necessary, they used smaller boats, which were light enough to be carried overland, to avoid bends in the river or rapids.

These trading expeditions were set up by groups of karls. Most of those who went could farm, row, sail, or fight as well as haggle for the best deal. The Vikings traded over a large area of the world, from the icy shores of Greenland, famous for its walrus ivory, to the bazaars of southwest Asia. They exchanged goods with many different peoples, such as Slavs, German and Baltic peoples, Franks, Anglo-Saxons, Greeks, and Arabs.

Goods could be bartered (exchanged) or paid for with bars of silver. Foreign coins were soon being used, too. They were sometimes cut into pieces and valued just by the weight of their silver. In the 900s CE, as Viking kings became more powerful, they began to make some of their own coins.

3-second sum-up

Ships allowed the Vikings to trade with many different peoples and over great distances.

3-minute mission Mint some money

You need: • Silver posterboard • Scissors • Thin-tipped black marker

Imagine you are a Viking king. You want to design and mint (make) some coins to show how powerful you are. The design might show a ship, an ax, or a sword. Cut out some coin-sized discs from silver posterboard, and draw on your designs with the marker.

The Vikings traded locally as well as in distant lands. They bartered for goods such as amber, wine, and tin or paid with silver bars and coins.

Germany provided swords of the finest quailty.

Scandinavia and Russia were centers of the fur trade.

Silks and spices were imported from Asia.

Goods were bartered, or exchanged, with other items.

Vikings sold fish, sulfur for fire-based weapons, and falcons for hunting.

Raids and plunder

... in 30 seconds

The Vikings used their fast longships to attack villages and towns along coasts and rivers. Today, we have lots of technology to warn us of an enemy attack. In the Viking Age, however, villagers scarcely had time to race from the fields back to their homes before the longships were beached and armed warriors were swarming ashore.

Viking raids were brief and brutal and the attackers could make a quick getaway using their boats. The local people were murdered or captured as slaves. Buildings were burned down. Cattle were stolen and grain stores were ransacked for food. The best plunder was items that were easy to carry—gold and silver, weapons, tools, clothes, furs, and jewelry.

The Vikings often targeted Christian monasteries. These were poorly defended, and the monks often had chests full of coins as well as precious crosses, plates, and bells. Sometimes the Vikings attacked other ships. Like most pirates, they avoided damaging these ships too much, because they wanted to steal and use them themselves. When the Vikings returned home, they shared out the loot and bragged about their daring deeds.

3-second sum-up

The Vikings raided coastal towns, villages, and monasteries, taking people and treasure.

Famous Viking raids

789 CE The Isle of Portland in Wessex (southern England).

793 CE The monastery at Lindisfarne, Northumbria (northeastern England).

794 CE The monastery at Iona, off Scotland. It is attacked again in 795 CE, 802 CE, and 806 CE.

795 CE Rathlin Island (off Antrim, Ireland) followed by the Irish kingdoms of Brega (798 CE) and Connacht (807 CE).

834–837 CE The Dutch town of Dorestad is destroyed four times.

834 CE The coastal defenses of the Franks are attacked.

852 CE First attack on Wales—the island of Anglesey is hit in 903 CE and 918 CE.

Violent raids were not unusual in Europe in the 800s CE. The Vikings were the most successful raiders because they had the best ships and were the best seafarers.

Villagers were seized as slaves.

Christian monks would try to run away from the pagan Vikings. Some were killed with swords and axes.

Raiders looted buildings and set them on fire with a burning arrow. They wanted to drive out anyone who was hiding inside.

Cattle and sheep were rounded up.

Settlers overseas

... in 30 seconds

Viking raids mostly took place in summer months, when the sailing was best. But as the raiders grew bolder, they began to spend winters overseas as well. They set up onshore bases or camps and defended them from attack. The Irish called these longphorts.

Longphorts could be used as temporary centers for raiding expeditions, or as trading posts. Some of them grew into permanent settlements, into towns or even small kingdoms such as Dublin and Limerick in Ireland.

Ships would bring whole families and households to new settlements. They came with weapons and with tools to build homes and grow crops. Some women were captured on raids around the British Isles and taken to Iceland to be wives of new settlers. Sometimes the Viking settlers mixed in with people already living in the region.

Why did Vikings settle overseas? Many wanted better farmland than they had at home. Some could not inherit property of their own. A few may have been forced into exile because of crimes they had committed at home.

3-second sum-up

Vikings began to settle in new lands, building homes and preparing the land for farming.

3-minute mission Norse detective

Vikings left traces of their language, Old Norse, in the names of islands, bays, towns, and buildings across many parts of the world. Here are some examples. Can you find any more on a map?

-ey or **-ay** = island, e.g. Bardsey (Wales), Olney (US)
-thwaite = meadow, e.g. Le Thuit (France)
-ness = headland, e.g. Inverness (Australia)
-by = settlement or farm, e.g. Whitby (England), Grimsby (Canada)
-vik = bay, e.g. Hoyvik (Faroe Islands), Reykjavik (Iceland)
-kirk = church, e.g. Ormskirk (England), Falkirk (Scotland)

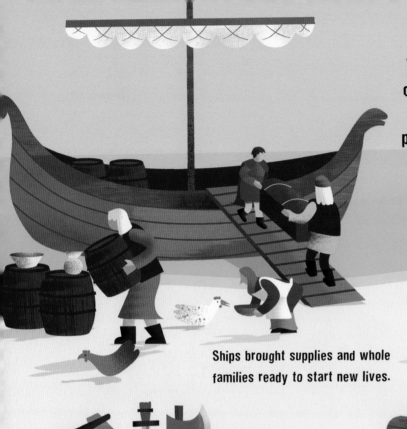

The settlers first built camps to live in before they made more permanent settlements.

Ships brought supplies and whole families ready to start new lives.

Swords and shields were kept on hand in case the settlers were attacked.

Vikings used local materials such as stone, timber, and turf for building new homes.

Viking tent poles sometimes had decorative carvings.

Vikings chose sites that had good access to the ocean, rivers, and clean freshwater.

Raiders and fighters

In an age before guns or bombs, warriors fought closely, person to person, and combat was brutal. In reality, the Vikings were no more violent than other peoples of their time, such as the Franks or the Anglo-Saxons. But the Christian monks of the day described the Vikings as fiendish fighters. Later on, Norse writers wrote down exciting stories about the Vikings, called sagas. These sagas described the warriors as adventurous and heroic. For both of these reasons, the Vikings are still remembered as some of the most famous warriors in history.

Raiders and fighters
Glossary

battering ram A length of heavy timber used to smash through the defenses of a fort or castle.

battle ax An ax designed for use as a weapon.

berserker A Viking warrior who went crazy during a battle, or a class or rank of warrior. Warriors wore the skin of a bear or wolf to gain the fighting power of an animal.

besiege To surround and cut off the enemy, so that they cannot receive supplies or get help.

boss A central stud on a shield, usually made of metal.

byrnie (brynja in Old Norse) A mail shirt, used as armor in battle.

catapult Any machine used in sieges to hurl missiles at the enemy.

close ranks To move closer to each other while in a battle formation.

Danegeld Money raised by a king to pay off Viking invaders.

Danevirke An earthwork designed to protect the southern borders of Denmark from attack.

double-edged Of a sword, sharp on both edges of the blade.

gatehouse The defensive entrance to a fort or town.

hilt The handle of a sword.

housecarl (húskarl in Old Norse) A bodyguard or warrior of the royal household.

inlaid Decorated by filling in spaces with another material, such as a precious metal.

karl A free male citizen in Viking society, able to trade and own property.

mail A protective fabric made of small, interlinked metal rings.

Middle Ages/medieval The period of European history, which separates the time of Ancient Rome from the modern world of discovery and science. Some historians date it from 476 CE to 1453.

pitched battle A formal battle at a given place, as opposed to a skirmish or running conflict.

rampart A defensive wall or bank.

raven A large black crow, associated with the Norse god Odin.

refuge A place that is safe from attack, a haven.

ring fort In the Viking period, a system of defenses used to encircle buildings.

saga Old Norse tales of adventures, voyages, and battles.

shaft The long stick or pole that forms the body of a spear or arrow.

shield wall A defensive battle formation, in which warriors stood shoulder to shoulder with their shields overlapping.

steel Iron that has been mixed with a tiny amount of carbon, from charcoal, to form a very hard material. It was used to forge blades.

Warriors

... in 30 seconds

Viking warriors were mostly ordinary karls, who were called away from farming to go to war. Sometimes they joined up with other groups to form larger forces, but only a few were full-time, paid soldiers. Viking warriors might march to battle, sail there in ships, or ride on horseback. Most of the fighting was on foot.

At the start of the battle, Viking archers might fire arrows at the enemy from powerful bows. Spears could be thrown or, as the fighters closed in on the enemy, used to jab and stab. Battle axes with curved blades were used to beat, hack, or hook enemies, cracking open helmets or smashing shields. The Viking sword was double-edged with a groove. It was forged from iron and edged in steel, and was used to slash at the enemy.

We read about warriors who went really crazy in battle, but we don't know much about them. They worked themselves up into a furious rage. They are often called berserkers, a word suggesting that they wore shirts made of bearskin. However, some historians think that the word "berserker" should actually refer to a top warrior or champion. Members of the king's personal bodyguard were called housecarls.

3-second sum-up

Most Viking men were part-time soldiers. They fought with bows, spears, axes, and swords.

3-minute mission Name that sword

Weapons were valuable possessions, handed down from father to son. The sword of a king or a jarl might have a richly decorated hilt. An iron ax blade might be inlaid with silver. Vikings liked to give their best weapons nicknames, such as "leg biter," "war flame," or "villain." Can you make up some good names for a Viking sword?

Combat was exhausting. The fighters had to leap, kick, lunge, and punch. All the time they were looking for an unguarded spot they could attack.

Sword blades were about 28–32 in long and edged in steel. Later Viking swords were longer.

A small ax weighed about 1.8 lbs.

Bows measured about 6 ft and had a range of up to 275 yds. The arrows had iron heads.

Spears had a shaft (the handle) of ash wood and an iron head. They were 7–10 ft long.

Battle axes had curved blades and the wooden shaft could be long or short.

Armor

... in 30 seconds

In the early Middle Ages, few northern European warriors wore heavy armor to protect themselves in battle. Most men fought in their everyday clothes, wearing tunics and pants. This gave them freedom to run and jump.

The richest Viking warriors might own a byrnie, a shirt of mail. This was made up of small, interconnected iron rings. Each ring was linked to the four closest to it.

Most iron helmets were round or conical, and padded inside with leather or sheepskin. They did not have horns, as shown so often in modern pictures! Some were fitted with a bar at the front, to protect the nose. The best helmets had a face guard, to protect the eyes and cheeks, or maybe some mail to cover the back of the neck.

Shields were used for defense, but could also be slammed into an opponent as a weapon of attack. They were made of wooden planks, rimmed and sometimes covered in leather. A central iron boss added strength and protected the handhold on the other side. Shields could be slung over the shoulder when not in use.

3-second sum-up

Viking armor included a simple iron helmet and, for those who could afford it, a mail shirt.

3-minute mission Make a shield

You need: • Heavy cardboard • Tape • Colored paints • Paintbrush

Viking shields were often painted in bright colors and bold patterns. Make a shield to fit your size by cutting out a large circle from heavy cardboard. Tape a cardboard handle on the back. On the front, paint the central boss in gray and around it add a colored pattern, maybe with swirls, quarters, stripes, or a cross.

Warriors could defend a position by closing ranks and standing shoulder-to-shoulder, with their shields overlapping. This was called a shield wall. It was very hard for the enemy to break through it.

A mail shirt weighed about 26 lbs. It had short sleeves and came down to the thigh.

Face guard

Nose bar

Leather rim

Shields were up to 3 ft across and weighed about 11-15 lbs.

Viking armies
... in 30 seconds

By the 840s CE, small groups of Viking raiders were joining together to fight in larger forces numbering up to a thousand or more. These armies might be led by a king. Sometimes Viking armies joined one foreign kingdom in order to fight another.

Viking armies were able to march inland and fight pitched battles with their enemies. They attacked France in the 840s CE and the Anglo-Saxon kingdoms of England during the years 866 to 878 CE. They invaded, occupied, and settled large areas of land.

Vikings in England and France found out that if they attacked the same place again and again, the enemy would give them money just to go away. In England this bribe later became known as Danegeld. The scheme never worked well for long for the defenders, because the Vikings would come back a few years later and demand even more.

Gradually, the enemies of the Vikings learned better ways of fighting back. Alfred the Great, the Anglo-Saxon king of Wessex from 871 to 899 CE, greatly improved defenses. He trained soldiers and built warships.

3-second sum-up

Vikings soon began to form large armies to attack cities, conquer new lands, or demand money from their enemies.

3-minute mission Fly the raven banner

You need: • Small amount of fabric • Scissors • Fabric paints • Bamboo stake

Some Viking armies flew a small battle flag with a picture of a raven. This bird was an emblem of the great god Odin, the lord of battle and death. To make a flag, cut out a triangle shape from the fabric, with a curved lower edge. Make small cuts into the curved edge to create tassels. Use fabric paints to draw the raven. Attach your battle flag to a bamboo stake.

Viking armies had enough warriors and weapons to attack or besiege places such as London, Paris, Ghent, or Hamburg.

Ships on the river brought supplies to the Vikings.

A catapult could hurl boulders to knock down the city walls.

Wooden towers were set on fire with flaming arrows.

A battering ram could smash down the city gates.

Walls and forts

... in 30 seconds

Walls, ditches, and fences were often built around towns to protect them from being attacked. Three hundred years before the Vikings, the Danes began work on a great wall—the Danevirke—to defend their homeland from attack by Franks and Saxons. This wall was made even better by Viking rulers such as King Gudfred in 808 CE.

The Danevirke stretched for 19 miles across Denmark, from the western wetlands to the eastern port of Hedeby, on the Baltic coast. In places it was up to 20 ft high. It was still being used as a defense in warfare over 1,000 years later, in 1864, and its remains stand today.

During the reign of Harald Bluetooth (about 958 to 986 CE), the Vikings built ring forts in Denmark and southern Sweden. Wooden buildings and streets were surrounded by ditches and a circular mound, faced with heavy timbers, soil, and stone. Each fort had gates in the north, south, east, and west. The best-known forts include Trelleborg and Fyrkat.

The Viking settlement at Dublin, Ireland, was protected by a bank made of mud and gravel, topped by a wooden fence. Later, the Vikings replaced this with a stone wall.

3-second sum-up

The Vikings built walls of soil, stone, and timber along borders and around their towns and forts.

An island fortress

The old Viking sagas tell of an awesome island fortress called Jomsborg. It had stone towers defended by catapults and a harbor sealed off by a great iron gate. The Jomsvikings who lived there were a wild bunch who offered up their services as warriors. Fact or fiction? Nobody can be sure, but some people believe the fortress did exist on the island of Wolin, in the southern Baltic Sea.

Vikings built ring forts to defend their towns and as places for the king's armies to be kept.

N

E

W

S

Timber-faced walls and ditches protected the people inside.

The walls had a gatehouse at the four points of a compass.

Ramparts

Guards

Messengers were sent on horseback to carry important news from the forts.

Forts may also have been gathering points or refuges in times of war, or used for collecting taxes in peacetime.

Everyday life

Away from the dangers of battle or the ocean waves, life carried on as normal for most Vikings. There were seasonal tasks to carry out on the farm, daily household chores, buying and selling at market, and babies to care for. The Vikings loved life, but it was a hard struggle for them. Almost everything had to be made by hand, and a lot of the work required hard labor and muscle power. If you had an accident or became sick, there were no medicines or hospitals either—just herbal remedies, or a charm to bring good luck.

Everyday life
Glossary

anvil The heavy iron block on which a blacksmith hammers hot metal into shape.

bellows A machine that puffs a blast of air into a fire, to make it burn more strongly.

cesspit A hole dug in the soil to dispose of sewage.

felt A fabric made by compacting wool fibers.

forge A smithy, a place for shaping and hammering hot metal.

griddle A flat, heated surface used for cooking.

hnefatafl A popular Viking board game. The name literally means fist table, but the game is better known as king's table. To pronounce it, see page 92.

kenning A poetic or alternative description of something or someone, which avoids using the normal term.

leg bindings Long narrow strips of cloth, sometimes wrapped around the leg and foot by Viking men.

linen A textile made from fibers of the flax plant.

loom The frame on which a textile is woven.

madder A plant with small yellow flowers, but with a long root used in preparing red dyes.

mead An alcoholic drink made from honey and water.

midden A garbage heap.

Middle Ages/medieval The period of European history that separates the time of ancient Rome from the modern world of discovery and science. Some historians date it from 476 to 1453 CE.

preserve To prepare food so that it remains edible, by drying, smoking, salting, or pickling.

saga A Norse story written down in the Middle Ages, telling of families, feuds, great ocean voyages, and adventures.

sedge A group of rushlike wetland plants.

shift A woman's dress or an under-dress, simple and unwaisted.

smithy A smith's workshop, where metal is hammered and forged.

soapstone A type of rock that is easy to carve. The Vikings used it to make cooking pots.

tanner Someone who soaks and treats animal hides to turn them into leather.

tapestry A textile woven as a work of art, usually hung on a wall for display.

walrus ivory The long, tusklike upper teeth of the walrus, used as a material from which objects were carved in the Viking period.

wattle and daub A building material made of interwoven wooden strips plastered with materials such as wet clay, dung, and straw.

weld A plant also known as dyer's rocket, with yellow-green flowers. It produces a bright yellow dye.

welding Joining together two pieces of metal, by heating, pressing, and hammering.

wick A strip of fiber inside a candle or oil lamp, which soaks up the fuel and burns.

woad A plant with yellow flowers. Its leaves produce a blue dye.

How to dress

... in 30 seconds

Viking clothes for men and women were colorful, and their fashions changed over time. Viking women and girls generally wore a long shift of linen, and over that a shorter dress or a jumper dress made of wool. This was held up by shoulder straps and fastened by brooches.

Glass or amber beads could hang in a loop between the two brooches. Keys, scissors, or other useful items were hung from a belt at the waist. A shawl, a cloak, or a fur might be worn on a cold night. Young girls wore their hair long and sometimes braided, or with combs made from antler horn. Married women wore their hair in a bun, under a headscarf.

Men and boys wore a tunic of linen under an outer tunic of wool, often trimmed with fancy braiding. Pants could be baggy or narrow, and sometimes leg bindings were wrapped around the calves. There were hooded cloaks, caps of wool, and fur hats. Men wore their hair long, and were expected to have a beard and moustache, kept neatly trimmed.

3-minute mission Make a brooch

A high-status Viking woman wore the very best brooches to show just how rich she was. Two oval brooches of bronze decorated the shoulder straps, while smaller brooches fastened cloaks and shawls. You can cut out brooch shapes from cardboard and paint with Viking animal designs from the Internet. Tape a safety pin to the back and wear with pride!

Spinning, weaving, and sewing were carried out by women in the home. Textiles were woven on a large, upright loom.

Linen shift

Woolen dress

Hair pin

Head scarf

Brooch to fasten shoulder straps

Children wore the same sort of clothing as their parents, just in smaller sizes.

Linen tunic

Woolen tunic

Woolen pants

Fur hat

Leather shoes, boots or slippers were made of calfskin or goatskin, and often worn with woolen socks.

Farming life

... in 30 seconds

In Viking times there were few actual roads. People walked along rough tracks through the countryside. Some rode small, tough horses, or used them for carrying packs of goods. There were wooden wagons, and in winter, travelers could use sleds, skates, or skis.

Most Vikings lived by farming the land. In warmer areas where the soil was good, the farms were quite close to each other, sometimes forming villages. In colder regions with poor soil, there were fewer farms.

Farming settlements were home to land-owning families, free laborers and slaves. The main building was the longhouse (see pages 56–57). Around it there might be a wash-house, barns, cowsheds, a dairy, and a smithy.

Viking farmers grew rye, barley, and oats, which could be ground into flour with a round stone. In warmer regions they could plant wheat. Hay was grown to feed the animals. Cattle grazed on fresh grass on the hillsides during the summer. In the fall, they were brought down to the cow sheds. People preserved meats by drying, salting, or smoking them.

3-second sum-up

Farmers raised cattle, sheep, and pigs, and grew crops such as rye, barley, and oats.

3-minute mission What's it for?

All these tools might be found on a Viking farm. What do you think they were used for?

1. Sickle

2. Shears

3. Quern

See page 96 for answers.

Throughout the year, most Vikings spent their time looking after their animals and crops on farms.

In spring, farmers planted seeds of rye, barley, and oats.

In summer, the sheep were sheared to provide wool for clothing.

In the fall, the crops were harvested.

In the cold days of winter, cattle were kept in sheds or at one end of the longhouse and fed on hay.

Inside a longhouse

... in 30 seconds

At the center of the farmstead stood the longhouse, up to 32 to 66 yds long, and 16 to 23 ft wide. It was normally built from timber, with walls made of crisscrossed sticks plastered with mud or dung ("wattle and daub"). The roof was covered with straw or tiled with wood. In areas where wood was scarce, such as Iceland, the longhouse might be stone-built, with a roof of turf. As time passed, extra rooms might be added at the sides.

Indoors, rows of wooden posts held up the roof beams, dividing the interior into three aisles. The floor was made of packed soil and ash. The center of family life was the hearth. This was a firepit, which provided heating, light, and cooking. Smoke escaped through holes in the roof.

Wooden benches or ledges in the side aisles were used as seats and beds. Mattresses were filled with straw or feathers, and blankets or furs kept sleepers warm when winter storms roared over the roof. There was little furniture, but shields could be hung on the walls, and a wealthy landowner might decorate the walls with carvings or tapestries.

3-second sum-up

The longhouse was the center of family life, used for eating, sleeping, and tasks such as weaving.

Lamplight

It was dark inside a longhouse as there were no windows. Only a little light came from the fire, so the Vikings needed to use lamps. Simple lamps were made from stone containers filled with oil extracted from plants or the fat from fish, seals, or whales. The wick was made of cottongrass, a kind of sedge, which burned steadily. Modern oil lamps are based on the same idea.

56

A longhouse needed to be big to fit in a family, their relatives or guests, and farm workers. One end was sometimes also used to house farm animals in winter.

This ironing board is made of whalebone. Clothes were smoothed out with a ball of glass.

Chests, baskets, barrels, buckets, and hooks were used for storage.

The roof was covered with straw or turf.

Cauldrons were made of iron and hung on chains over the fire.

Mattresses were filled with straw or feathers.

Weaving area

Walls were made of wattle (crisscrossed sticks), which were plastered with daub (mud or straw mix) in between strong wooden posts.

Cooking area

Peat, brushwood or logs were burned in the firepit.

Food and feasts

... in 30 seconds

Family meals were eaten mid-morning and in the evening. Oats, barley, or rye were used to make porridge or a coarse bread, which could be baked on an iron or stone griddle. Cheese was made from the milk of sheep, goats, and cows.

Leeks, onions, turnips, cabbages, and peas were grown in the fields. Herrings were a big part of the diet, whether freshly caught, smoked, or salted. Honey was used to sweeten meals. Meat might be roasted, but more often it was boiled or stewed. Beef, pork, mutton, goat, or chicken were all eaten. Even horse meat was eaten until the Vikings became Christian, when it was banned because it was associated with Pagan festivals.

Hunting in the woods and fields brought in hare, deer, elk, boar, and wildfowl, and useful plant foods such as berries and nuts. Seabird eggs were collected from cliffs.

The Vikings ate from bowls or plates made of wood, using knives or daggers, and spoons made of wood or horn—but no forks. Their dishes were made from a type of rock called soapstone. Pottery cups and jugs were often imported from Germany, along with wine.

3-second sum-up

The Viking diet included coarse bread, stewed vegetables, fish, and meat.

3-minute mission Viking snacks

We don't really have any Viking recipes, but we do know which foods they ate. Your mission is to prepare some healthy food for a hungry Viking friend! In a bowl, mix up some oats, apple slices, blueberries, hazelnuts, milk, and honey. On the side you could provide a whole wheat bun with some cheese. Ask your friend to eat it using a spoon!

Chiefs or jarls liked to entertain guests and enjoyed feasting and drinking. A seasonal festival or a family celebration could last for days.

Drinking horn

"Ves heil" means "Your good health!" in Old Norse.

Meat was usually boiled or stewed.

Barley bread

Cheese

Fruit

Herring and vegetables

Eggs

Soapstone dishes

Wooden cup

Wooden plate

Strong drinks included ale, made from barley, and mead, made from honey. Wine was imported from Germany.

Living in a town
... in 30 seconds

In much of Europe, big cities had been built by the Romans. Regions such as Scandinavia, though, which lay outside the Roman Empire, did not develop a city lifestyle. Instead, smaller but busy towns such as Hedeby, Germany, which had a population of about 1,000—2,000, grew up from the 700s and 800s CE.

Viking towns were often ocean or river ports, and were centers for making and trading goods. Inside the town's defenses, the streets were paved with lengths of heavy timber. There were market stalls, probably selling everything from fresh fish to hammers and nails. Ships were moored at jetties in the harbor.

Houses were built of timber beams with walls of planking or wattle and daub. They were similar inside to a longhouse. Some buildings had sunken cellars, which were probably used as warehouses or workshops. Household garbage was tipped onto middens, and sewage was buried in cesspits. There wasn't any good drainage.

3-second sum-up

Viking towns were small but busy centers of craft and trade. Many of them were ports.

Timeline: Viking towns

700s CE Ribe is founded, a trading center in Jutland. It still exists and is Denmark's oldest town.

750s CE Birka in Sweden becomes the western end of trade routes into Russia. Today it is Sweden's oldest town.

780s CE Kaupang is a center of craft and trade in Norway. The name means "marketplace." Aarhus is founded at about the same time.

804 CE The first mention of Hedeby, on the border between Danish and German lands.

870 CE Viking settlers found Reykjavík, the capital of Iceland.

Towns often started as busy ports and began to grow larger in the 800s CE. A few survived and became the big cities of today.

The land was fenced off into plots, with sheds, gardens, and farm animals.

Jetty

Streets were paved with timber.

Traders and market stalls.

There were no windows but holes in the roof let out smoke.

Front doors faced the street.

A typical townhouse measured about 39 by 16 ft, but a rich merchant's house could be much bigger.

Growing up

... in 30 seconds

You needed to be lucky to grow up at all in the early Middle Ages. Many mothers died giving birth, and infants often died from illnesses that could not be cured. At the Viking settlement of Jórvik (York, in England), probably one in three babies never reached adulthood.

Nine days after the birth, the father placed the baby on his knee and sprinkled the head with water. He or she was given a name and recognized as a member of the family. Guests brought gifts to the ceremony.

Boys and girls were expected to work hard. They would help on the farm or in the workshop, spinning wool, mending clothes, taking care of younger siblings or animals, fishing, or cutting wood. There were no schools or formal lessons. Children might be fostered out to another family, to strengthen social ties or to learn a new skill.

At 12 a boy was already taking on adult tasks, and at 15 he could go off raiding. A girl would marry in her early teens. Marriages were generally arranged as business deals or alliances between families.

3-minute mission Make a bouncy felt ball

You need: • Some wool strands • A bowl • Dishwashing soap

1. Mix 4 tablespoons of dishwashing soap with 6 cups of warm water in a bowl.
2. Scrunch up a small ball of woolen fiber with your hand, then wind strands around it. When your ball is twice as big as the one you want, dip it in the water. Keep rolling it between the palms of your hands for 10 minutes, without squeezing.
3. When it has shrunk, rinse it under cold water and let it dry. Tie some colored woolen yarn around it and let it bounce!

Viking children had to grow up quickly and learn skills such as swimming, farm work, and sword fighting, to help them set up new communities when they grew up.

Toddlers played with dolls, toy animals, or balls made of felt.

Young children fought with pretend swords made of wood to prepare for real sword fights.

As children got older, they were expected to work hard in the longhouse and on the farm.

By the age of 15, boys were old enough to go off on raids.

Girls got married once they reached their early teens.

Fun and games

... in 30 seconds

Men loved sports such as wrestling, tug-of-war, weight-lifting, skating, and swimming. There were bat-and-ball games, too. Most sports were played to the extreme and often ended in violence.

Board games were always very popular. Viking families played dice, chess, checkers, and games similar to backgammon. One game was called "hnefatafl." Players had to protect their king while he tried to escape to his corner castles.

Little is known about how the Vikings danced or played music, but we do know that they played pipes and flutes made from bone or horn, and stringed instruments, including a harp. Ibrahim al-Tartushi, a traveler from Spain, visited Hedeby in 965 CE. He said that Viking songs sounded like dogs or wild animals howling!

The Vikings loved words, especially riddles, rhymes, and poems. Traveling poets called skalds would attend the feast of a jarl or a king and compose verse to music. In the long winter evenings, stories of gods, giants, tricksters, trolls, heroes, and kings were told around the fire. Later in the Middle Ages, longer stories called sagas were written down in books.

3-second sum-up

The Vikings liked extreme outdoor sports as well as board games, music, and storytelling.

3-minute mission Word puzzles

Viking poets liked to use kennings—phrases that described something without directly saying what it was. The listener had to work out the meaning. The Sun might be called a "sky-candle." The wind might be called a "tree-breaker." Can you make up some modern kennings? For example, a motorcycle could be a "fast-lane snarler." How about inventing a kenning for a smartphone?

Vikings liked to entertain themselves with music, singing, wrestling, and playing board games.

Wrestling was a popular sport, but it could get violent.

Scandinavian music of the early Middle Ages was not written down. It remains a mystery.

Horn

Flute

Stringed instrument

These Viking chess pieces were found on the Isle of Lewis in Scotland. They were carved from walrus ivory in the 1100s CE.

Tales of magic and heroic adventures were told around the fire.

Arts and crafts

... in 30 seconds

In the days before factories, it was individual craft workers who made the things that people used, bought, or sold every day. In a Viking town there might be carpenters, tanners of leather, shoemakers, and glassmakers. Woodturners used lathes to shape wooden bowls and poles. At home, potters made jugs, pots, loom weights, and oil lamps.

A blacksmith worked with metal and was probably the most important craft worker of all. He worked in a forge, using bellows to make the furnace burn hot, so that the metal could be shaped into nails, knives, axes, keys, pots, and pans. Swordsmiths might take a week or more to fashion a blade, twisting iron rods, welding, and hammering.

Other metalworkers and jewelers used precious materials such as silver or gold. They worked with beautiful glass and amber beads to make rings, necklaces, and bracelets.

Carvers worked on all sorts of surfaces, such as horn, walrus ivory, whale tooth, antler, or soapstone. Carved wood decorated houses, furniture, ships, wagons, and, later, churches. Favorite Viking patterns included interlaced knots and loops, birds and fish, beasts, and dragons. These designs influenced those of other peoples such as the Anglo-Saxons and the Irish.

3-second sum-up

Craftworkers made tools, weapons, and household goods as well as beautiful carvings and delicate jewelry.

Bright colors

Viking textiles and tapestries were brightly colored with dyes made from plants. The leaves of the woad plant turned cloth blue. The husks of walnuts produced a brown. The root of a plant called madder made things red. The flowers of weld, or dyer's rocket, gave a yellow dye, while heather stems were used for dark green.

The Vikings were skilled craftspeople, particularly blacksmiths who turned metal into useful objects.

First the iron is heated and then hammered flat.

Bellows make the fire really hot, so that the iron becomes softer.

The hot, soft iron is hammered into shape.

The item is cooled off in a bucket of water.

Blacksmiths made essential things such as swords, nails, and keys.

Silversmiths from Jutland made this brooch.

This carved woodwork animal head was found in Norway.

This Swedish tapestry was made on a loom.

Religion and beliefs

Before the Vikings became Christian, they had myths to explain the origins of the world and the meaning of life and death. The Vikings believed there was a human world (Midgard) and a home of the gods (Asgard) connected by a shimmering rainbow bridge, called Bifröst. In all there were nine such worlds inhabited by humans and all sorts of other beings, such as gods, elves, dwarfs, giants, and dragons. This universe was held together by the roots of a gigantic ash tree called Yggdrasil. These old myths and legends survived even after Christianity came to the Viking lands, in the 800s CE.

Religion and beliefs
Glossary

Aesir One of the two groups of Norse gods. The Aesir included **Odin** and **Thor**.

Asgard The home of the **Aesir** gods, one of the nine worlds of Norse mythology.

Baldr A god associated with love, peace, justice, and the Sun; the son of **Odin** and the goddess **Frigg**.

burial mound A pile of earth marking a tomb or grave.

Freyja A goddess of love and beauty; the twin sister of **Freyr**.

Freyr A fertility god of the **Vanir**, who lives in Álfheim, the world of the elves.

Frigg A powerful goddess of wisdom; the wife of **Odin**.

Landvaettir Spirits of the countryside and nature.

Loki A god known for making mischief, who can change shape and take the form of an animal.

Midgard In Norse myths, the middle world where human beings live.

missionary Someone sent to spread a religious message and convert people to their faith.

myth An ancient tale of gods, goddesses, heroes, or monsters, heaven or hell. It aims to explain the meaning of life or why things happen as they do.

Norns Female beings who visit babies to decide how their lives will work out in the future.

Odin The greatest and the most powerful of the **Aesir** gods. Odin is the god of battle, death, healing and knowledge.

pagan A person who follows a pre-Christian or non-Christian faith.

pyre A large, open wood fire, used to burn bodies during a funeral.

sacrifice Killing an animal or a person as an offering to a god or gods.

solstice When the Sun is at its greatest distance from the equator—in the summer, this is the longest day of the year and, in the winter, it is the shortest.

stave church A stave is a strip of wood. Stave churches, made of timber planks and tiled with wood, were made by the first Christians in Scandinavia.

superstitious Believing in supernatural causes being responsible for everyday events.

Thor A god of the **Aesir**, linked with thunder and lightning. The son of **Odin**, he fights giants with his hammer.

Valhalla (Valhöll in Old Norse) **Odin's** great hall in **Asgard**, the home of warriors killed in battle.

Vanir One of the two groups of Norse gods, including **Freyr** and **Freyja**. After a war, the Vanir became a subgroup of the **Aesir**.

Yggdrasil In Norse myths, the great ash tree that supports the nine worlds of the universe.

Yule (Jól in Old Norse) The pagan winter festival of the Vikings and other Germanic peoples. It later became taken over by Christmas.

Gods and goddesses
... in 30 seconds

According to some Norse myths, there were originally two tribes of gods and goddesses. The Aesir were associated with power and war and the Vanir were associated with wisdom, nature, magic, and fertility. The two tribes fought each other before they joined together.

The chief of the gods was called Odin and he belonged to the Aesir. He only had one eye and rode across the stormy sky on his eight-legged horse Sleipnir. He owned two wolves called Geri and Freki. His two ravens, Hugin and Munin, flew around the world to bring him news. Odin lived in a great hall called Valhöll. Warriors who died bravely in battle were taken there to feast with the gods.

The most popular god was red-headed Thor, the thunderer, who wielded a mighty war hammer. Freyr and Freyja were twins, the god and goddess of fertility and love. Baldr was god of the summer sun. Nothing could injure him, except an arrow made from mistletoe wood. His blind brother killed him with one. As usual, one god was at the root of this trouble—Loki, the mischief maker.

3-second sum-up

The Viking gods and goddesses included the great Odin, Thor the god of thunder, and Freyja the goddess of love.

3-minute mission Days of the week

In English and some other languages, some days of the week are still named after the old Viking and Germanic gods. See if you can work out which day of the week is named after these:

Anglo-Saxon god	Norse god	Day
Woden	Odin	?
Tiw	Tyr	?
Frige	Frigg	?
Thunre (Thunder)	Thor	?

See page 96 for answers.

Here are some of the many Viking gods and goddesses:

Gungnir was Odin's magic spear that never missed its target.

Odin had two ravens.

Sleipnir was Odin's eight-legged horse.

Odin had two wolves Geri and Freki.

Odin was chief of the gods.

Thor was the god of thunder.

Loki was the mischief maker.

Thor's hammer Mjöllnir was forged by dwarves.

Freyr and Freyja, the god and goddess of fertility and love.

The cats Bygul and Trjegul pulled Freyja's chariot.

Freyr had a boar called Gullinbursti.

Customs and festivals

... in 30 seconds

The Vikings' belief in spirits, gods, and goddesses was rooted in everyday life. The goddess Frigg ruled over weddings and marriage. That was why Vikings got married on Frigg's Day, or Friday. It was also thought that the fate of humans was decided at birth, by female beings called Norns.

The Vikings sometimes sacrificed animals and even humans to please the gods. Some religious rituals may have taken place outside, beside special trees or rocks, or in wooden buildings.

Vikings celebrated the passing of the seasons with sacrifices, feasting, drinking, and fire festivals. Later, the Christian church took over many old pagan customs, adapting them to the new faith. When the midwinter festival of Yule (Jól) was replaced by Christmas, Vikings carried on bringing a great log of oak into the house to start the New Year's fire. Some people still decorate their houses with plants at Christmas time, as the Vikings did long ago.

It is thought the Vikings celebrated May Day and midsummer day, too. In Sweden, people continue the May Day tradition by lighting bonfires and singing songs to welcome the return of warmth and light.

3-second sum-up

The Vikings held seasonal festivals, marked by sacrifices, feasting, and fire. Some still survive today.

3-minute mission Lucky charms

You need: • Self-drying clay • Silver paint • Paintbrush • String

The Vikings believed that wearing charms, such as a "Thor's hammer" symbol or an image of the goddess Freyja, would bring good luck. Make your own hammer (see drawing above) or a Freyja figure from clay. Leave a hole so that you can string it around your neck. Paint it silver when dry.

The Vikings held festivals throughout the year to honor their spirits, gods, and goddesses.

In the winter, Vikings decorated their houses with evergreen plants.

In midsummer, Vikings may have made bonfires to celebrate the solstice. They would sing songs and dance.

In the fall, animal sacrifice, known as a blot, took place to please the gods.

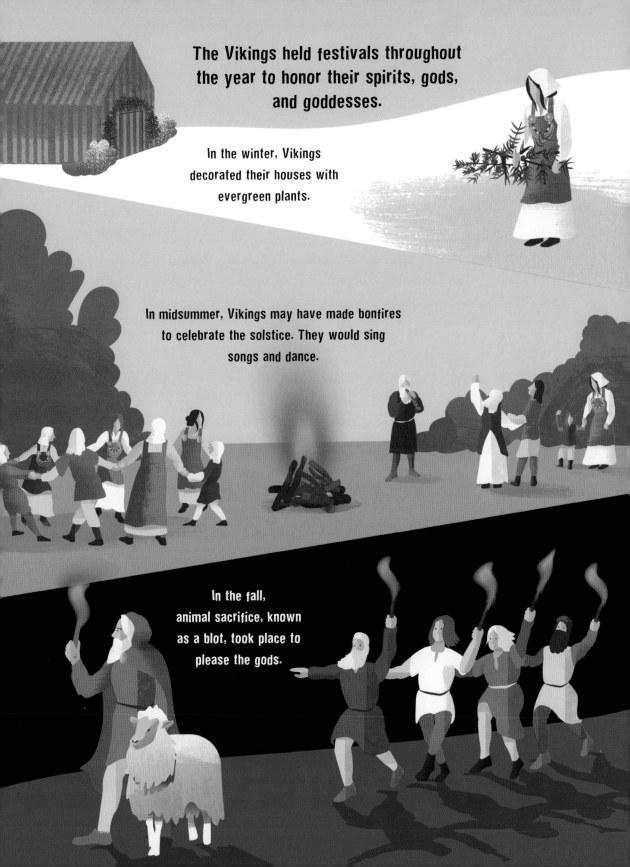

Viking funerals

... in 30 seconds

Death was never far away in the Viking period. Disease, warfare, and giving birth meant that many people died young. Those men and women who survived into their fifties were considered old.

Funerals varied greatly between regions and from one period to the next. Some Vikings were cremated on open fires or pyres after they died. Most were buried in the ground, in simple graves or under a mound.

Vikings were often buried with their possessions, so they would have everything they might need in their next life. The grave of one blacksmith contained all the hammers and tongs from his forge. The rich and powerful were given their best weapons or their finest clothes and jewelry. Some were buried with the sacrificed bodies of their slaves, and animals such as horses and dogs.

Kings and queens were sometimes buried in finely carved wagons with their best horses, or in beautiful longships. It isn't known whether these were seen as transportation to other worlds, or just as impressive symbols of worldly wealth and power.

3-second sum-up

Vikings were cremated or buried in the ground along with their favorite things.

The Oseberg ship

A beautiful ship was excavated by archeologists in Norway over 100 years ago. It had stayed buried under a mound of dirt since the year 843 CE. It was made of oak and decorated with carvings. Inside were the skeletons of two women, one in a very fine dress and linen veil. Also in the ship were richly carved sleighs and a wagon, a bed post, textiles, and tapestries.

Vikings were often buried with their possessions in simple graves or under a mound.

In some places stones were placed around the grave in the shape of a ship.

Burial mounds were later seen as spooky places. People were afraid they might meet the spirits of the undead.

Rich Vikings were buried with everything they might need in their next life.

The coming of Christianity

... in 30 seconds

By the start of the Viking Age, most people in western Europe had become followers of the Christian faith and believed in the teachings of Jesus Christ, but Vikings still held on to their own beliefs. These religious differences sometimes caused trading disputes and battles.

Many Vikings who had settled overseas soon became Christian. Some thought the Christian God brought prosperity and good fortune. Some were forced to convert after they had been defeated in battle. In the 700s and 800s CE, Christian missionaries traveled to Scandinavia to preach the new faith and build churches.

For many years pagan and Christian beliefs existed side by side in the Viking lands. Some new Christians still prayed to Thor in an emergency. King Harald Bluetooth, who ruled from Jelling, in Denmark, became a Christian in 960 CE. Later pictures show him being baptized in a barrel of water, by a monk called Poppo. During the 1000s CE Christianity spread through the Viking lands, but some people resisted and still made sacrifices to the old gods.

3-second sum-up

The Christian religion took about 300 years to take the place of the old pagan beliefs of the Vikings.

Pagan beliefs today

Viking settlers in Iceland believed that the countryside was protected by spirits known as Landvaettir, who lived in the rocks and fields. People said that the Landvaettir hated violence, so longship chiefs approaching Iceland would take down their dragon heads so as not to upset them. Belief in these spirits still exists today, and Icelanders protect particular sites from being disturbed by builders or farm workers. Four Landvaettir "protectors" appear on the back of modern Icelandic coins and Iceland's coat-of-arms.

Missionaries spread Christianity across Viking lands, though some Vikings held onto their pagan beliefs.

828 CE

The Christian missionary Ansgar visits Birka, Sweden.

960 CE

The Danish King Harald Bluetooth becomes a Christian.

1000 CE

The lawspeaker in Iceland judged that Christianity should be adopted (after thinking about it for a day under a cloak), but allowed people to carry on practicing the pagan religion.

995 CE

King Olaf Tryggvason builds the first church in Norway. He tries to force his people to convert to Christianity.

Christianity spreads in Norway under King Olaf II.

1015 CE

Most of Sweden is now Christian. The last pagan king dies in 1087 CE. Pagan customs are banned in Sweden in 1100 CE.

The wider world

The proof that the Vikings had been great travelers and settlers can be found in the hoards of Viking treasure that are still being discovered today. They include coins, jewelry, gold, and silver. Sometimes these items had been traded legally, but often they had been looted during raiding. One hoard was found in a bog at Hoen, Norway, in 1834. It contained items from France, Russia, England, the Byzantine Empire and the lands of the Arabs. The Spillings Hoard, found in Sweden in 1999, included 14,295 coins, which were mostly from Muslim lands.

The wider world
Glossary

Danelaw The area of Anglo-Saxon England that was taken over, settled, and governed by the Vikings.

dynasty A family in which rule or power is handed down from one generation to the next.

elite A superior or special group of people with high social standing.

Frankish Of the Franks, a people living in France during the early Middle Ages. They gave their name to the country.

hoard A secret store of money or valuable objects.

housecarl (húskarl in Old Norse) A bodyguard or warrior of the royal household.

Inuit A people of Arctic North America. Archeologists describe such peoples living there in Viking times as belonging to the Dorset and Thule cultures. The Vikings called them "skraelings."

legacy Something that has been handed down from the past to later generations.

Markland An area of the North American coast, probably Labrador in Canada, identified by Leif Eiriksson.

mercenary A soldier who hires himself out, fighting for money.

Miklagard The Vikings' name for Constantinople (Istanbul). It means "the great city."

Rus A people who traded and built up new towns in Eastern Europe, giving their name to Russia. They may have been Vikings or Slavs.

Up Helly Aa A winter fire festival held in Shetland, Scotland, celebrating the memory of Viking settlement.

Varangian Guard An elite guard founded in 988 CE to protect the Byzantine emperors. It was mostly made up of Vikings, but with some Anglo-Saxons and Germans.

Varangians The name given to Vikings from Sweden by the Slavs and the Greeks.

Vinland An area of the North American coast, probably Newfoundland in Canada, identified by Leif Eiriksson.

Western Europe

... in 30 seconds

The Vikings reached much of western Europe to trade, settle, or do battle. Few rivers, islands or coasts around the North Sea, the Irish Sea, or the English Channel were safe from their dragon ships.

The Vikings' largest area of settlement was across central and northern England, which became known as the Danelaw. Southern Anglo-Saxon cities such as London were also attacked. After 1016 CE, under King Cnut, England became, for a time, part of the Danish empire. In 1066 CE Harald Hardrada, King of Norway, tried to invade England but was defeated.

The lands that are now called Germany, France, the Netherlands, and Belgium were also plagued by Viking attacks. The Vikings besieged Paris in 845 CE and again from 885 to 886 CE. In despair, the Frankish kings gave away the region of Normandy to the Viking chief Hrólfr or Rollo in 911 CE. Brittany was also attacked by Vikings time after time.

The Vikings sailed down stormy Atlantic coasts and into the warm, blue waters of the Mediterranean Sea. They attacked Seville and other cities in Muslim Spain. In the 860s CE, a Viking fleet captured the island of Sicily.

3-second sum-up

The Vikings overran large areas of Britain and Ireland and attacked the mainland and the islands of western Europe.

Raids and invasions in western Europe

780s–790s CE France and England raided.

830s CE Viking attacks on the Netherlands. The first of many raids on London, England.

840s CE Raids in Scotland and Ireland, the settlement at Dublin. Attacks on Portugal and Spain, raiding the Muslim city of Seville. Major assaults on Hamburg and Paris.

860s CE Italy raided. Large areas of England are settled.

885–886 CE Northern France attacked, and Paris is besieged.

1013 CE Sweyn Forkbeard invades England.

Viking raiding and settlement was at its most intense in northwestern Europe, but their fleets also sailed along Atlantic and Mediterranean coasts.

Scandinavia

They fought with the peoples of England and Ireland.

Scots and Picts

North Sea

Gaels

· Dublin

Anglo-Saxons

· Hamburg

· London

They attacked northern France and besieged Paris.

Atlantic Ocean

Frankish warrior

The Vikings traded and fought with many other people living in northern Europe at that time.

Western Europe

Bay of Biscay

They fought with Moorish warriors in Muslim Spain.

· Cordoba

· Seville

North Atlantic

... in 30 seconds

The Vikings sailed west and reached the Faroe Islands, which are north of Scotland, in about 800 CE. They settled here to fish and raise sheep. In 874 CE Norse seafarers sailed on further to Iceland. The only previous settlers there had been a few Irish monks. The newcomers built farms on the best land and fished the seas. They loved to tell stories in the Icelandic language.

A seafarer called Gunnbjörn Ulfsson, who had been blown off course in a storm, was the first Viking to sight Greenland. This huge Arctic island was first settled permanently by Eirik the Red in about 982 CE. He called it Greenland to attract more settlers, but really it was a bleak and icy place inhabited by scattered Inuit communities. Settlers scraped a living by farming and hunting seals.

In about 1003 CE Eirik's son Leif "the Lucky" sailed to North America and landed at Labrador, which he called "Markland," and Newfoundland, or "Vinland." The Vikings bartered goods and sometimes fought with the North American tribes who lived there. Remains of Viking buildings and artifacts have been found at L'Anse aux Meadows, in the north of Newfoundland.

3-second sum-up

The Vikings sailed westward to the Faroe Islands, Iceland, Greenland, and North America.

Raids and invasions in the far north

800 CE Vikings settle on the Faroe Islands.

874 CE Vikings explore and settle Iceland.

982 CE Eirik "the Red" settles at Brattahlid, in Greenland.

c.986 CE Seafarer Bjarni Herjolfsson sights the mainland coast of North America.

1000s CE Leif Eiriksson "the Lucky" explores Labrador.

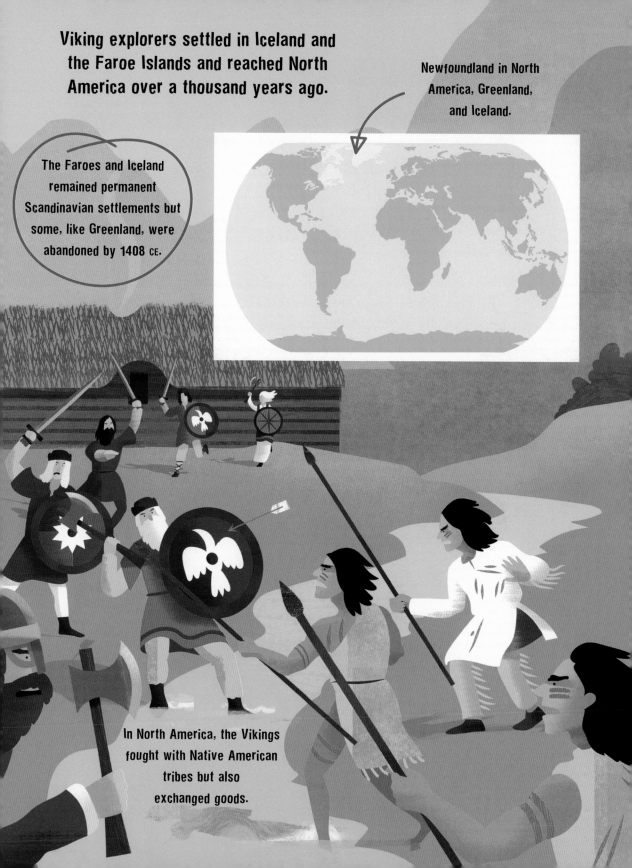

Eastern lands

... in 30 seconds

Swedish Vikings sailed across the Baltic Sea to raid the coast of Finland. They traveled into Russia, to Lake Ladoga and Novgorod. They traded in furs, amber, beeswax, honey, and slaves. They rowed down the great rivers of central and eastern Europe, to the Black Sea. The Greeks and Slavs called these Vikings "Varangians."

Some historians believe that a people known as the Rus, who gave their name to Russia, were Varangians. Their legendary chieftain, Rurik, is said to have founded a royal dynasty in 862 CE. Other historians disagree, but it is clear that both Varangians and Slavs helped to shape the future of eastern Europe.

Varangians traveled to the Caspian Sea and overland to Baghdad. From there, trading routes stretched eastwards all the way to China. The northerners traded with the Arabs for textiles and silver.

In the 900s CE some Vikings hired themselves out as mercenaries, to protect the Byzantine emperors. They were known as the Varangian Guard and they became an elite force, taking part in many famous battles and adventures. They were based at Constantinople (previously Byzantium and now modern-day Istanbul), which they called "the great city"—Miklagard.

3-second sum-up

The Vikings traveled into eastern Europe, traded in the markets of the Middle East, and fought for the Byzantine emperors.

Raids and invasions in the east

800s CE The town of Birka in Sweden is the start of trading routes in eastern Europe and Asia.

859 CE Novgorod in Russia is a major trading center for the Swedish Vikings or "Varangians."

862 CE Rurik founds a royal dynasty, which rules a large state called Kievan Rus.

911 CE Varangians fight as mercenaries for the Byzantines.

The Swedish Vikings moved eastward into Finland and Russia, and from there southward into Asia.

Finland and Russia

The Vikings traded in...

amber

silver

fur

slaves

They rowed down
rivers to trade
with Arabs.

Some Vikings hired themselves
out as mercenaries.

End of the Viking Age

... in 30 seconds

During the 1000s CE, Europe was going through many changes. Small kingdoms and territories were uniting under powerful kings. The Vikings were becoming Christian. Danes, Norwegians, and Swedes went on to play an important part in European history, but many Viking settlements overseas became swallowed up by new kingdoms such as England, France, or Scotland.

In France, the Normans still showed Viking spirit though. They sailed off to conquer Sicily and southern Italy, and in 1066 CE they crossed the English Channel to conquer England.

The Normans built great castles, and new warriors called knights, who were heavily armored and on horseback, were used to defend them instead of the housecarls fighting behind shields.

The Vikings left behind a rich legacy. This included language, styles of art and design, storytelling, boatbuilding, exploration, assemblies, and parliaments. A thousand years later, everyone still wants to know about the Vikings' battles, adventures, and ways of living.

3-second sum-up

The Viking Age came to an end as powerful Christian kingdoms emerged in Europe. New ways of fighting were developed by the Normans.

3-minute mission Viking names

Today, there are still people whose last names are based on the Viking system. Vikings identified babies as "son of" or "daughter of" their father. This is how it worked:

Eirik (= ever-powerful) **Thorvaldsson** (= son of Thorvald) **"the Red"** or **Sigrid** (= beautiful victory) **Tostadottir** (= daughter of Tosti) **"the Proud."**

Vikings loved giving people nickames, too—often funny or rude ones! Try giving yourself one, such as James son-of-Tom "the Nerd," or Lily daughter-of-Steve "the Blue Haired."

The Vikings' way of life still has an influence on our modern lives.

Traditional Viking styles of boatbuilding are still used to make a type of rowing boat called a skiff.

Up Helly Aa is a festival held in Shetland, Scotland, introduced in the 1800s to celebrate Viking traditions by burning a Viking-style ship and carrying torches in a procession.

Many of the days of the week are based on Viking and Anglo-Saxon names.

Sun Mon Tues Wed Thur Fri Sat

Some modern parliamentary traditions can be traced back to the Viking assemblies.

Icelandic assembly building called the Alpingishús.

Discover more

FICTION BOOKS

The Shield Ring
by Rosemary Sutcliff
Penguin, 1992

*The Viking Sagas: 1 Bracelet
of Bones; 2 Scramasax*
by Kevin Crossley-Holland
Quercus Children's Books, 2012

Thor and the Master of Magic
by Kevin Crossley-Holland
Barrington Stoke, 2013

MYTHS AND LEGENDS

Illustrated North Myths
by Alex Frith and Louie Stowell
Usborne, 2013

Norse Myths and Legends
by Anita Ganeri
Raintree, 2013

NON-FICTION BOOKS

100 Facts: Vikings
by Fiona Macdonald
Miles Kelly Publishing, 2008

Eyewitness: Viking
by Susan M Margeson
Dorling Kindersley, 2011

Greatest Warriors: Vikings
by Philip Steele
Arcturus Publishing 2013–2014

The Vicious Vikings by Terry Deary
Scholastic, 1998

ACTIVITY BOOKS

Hands on History: Vikings – Dress, Eat, Write and Play – just like the Vikings
by Fiona Macdonald
QED, 2011

Sigurd the Dragonslayer
by Dr. Ragnhild Ljosland
The Orcadian, 2014

WEBSITES

BBC resources
http://www.bbc.co.uk/history/ancient/vikings/

http://www.bbc.co.uk/education/topics/ztyr9j6

https://www.youtube.com/watch?v=taVsvYWp1UU

Information from Viking centers
http://jorvik-viking-centre.co.uk/who-were-the-vikings/

http://www.ribevikingecenter.dk/en/home.aspx

Viking game, National Museum of Scotland
http://www.nms.ac.uk/explore/games/vikings-training-school/

General reference
http://www.hurstwic.org/history/text/history.htm

To hear an Icelander pronounce hnefatafl
http://forvo.com/word/hnefatafl/

Although every endeavor has been made by the publisher to ensure that all content from these websites is educational material of the highest quality and is age appropriate, we strongly advise that Internet access is supervised by a responsible adult.

Index

Answers

Page 14: Crack the code!
THIS FISH IS A SHARK
THAT IS ITS FIN

Page 72: Days of the week

Tiw	Tyr	Tuesday
Woden	Odin	Wednesday
Thunre	Thor	Thursday
Frige	Frigg	Friday

Page 54: What's it for?
1. Sickle—Cutting corn
2. Shears—Cutting sheep's coats
3. Quern—Grinding grains